FOR MY WOMAN...

And You Thought I Didn't Understand

By

L. J. Flood

To Lisa - Thanks so much for allowing me to "try" to understand enjoy - [signature] 2004

ISBN: 1-4107-0113-1 (e-book)
ISBN: 1-4107-0114-X (Paperback)

Library of Congress Control Number: 2002096364

This book is printed on acid free paper.

Printed in the United States of America
Bloomington, IN

1stBooks - rev. 02/11/03

✠ DEDICATION ✠

This selection of poems is dedicated to:

My mother, Gladys,
My Wife, Patrice,
My daughter, Lavinia,
My sisters, Marilyn, Darlene, Denise, & Tina
And to all of those women
Who thought that they were
Alone...

And to all of those men
That attempted to make them feel
Otherwise.

To Chaz, my son.... you are greater than you think -

To sisters

Bertina & Joanne...

We are from
the same mold
and yet,
so distant.

WIFE DEDICATION
(To Patrice)

I took on

a wife

I took on

a friend

I took on

a whole new life

All over again.

♋ CONTENTS ∞

SISTER'S LAMENT

BROTHER'S LAMENT

FOR MY WOMAN

FOREWORD

"The hallmark of successful relationships is communication. One cannot communicate unless he or she knows what to communicate about and then can find the words with which to communicate. Well, look no farther. Mr. Flood does an amazing job at both identifying the various aspects of relationships about which to communicate, and finding the words with which to express those feelings. This, therefore, makes **For My Woman...And You Thought I Didn't Understand** a must read. Thank you, Mr. Flood."

Deborah P. Harrell, Ed.D.
Columbia University, Teachers College

FOREWORD II

"How beautiful it is
that you are willing to share your inner-self –
your vulnerability and passion –
without fear – risking rejection.
What strength of character it takes
to expose the beauty of your soul to another
through poetry.
You have something special –
not found often in men –
a willingness to be who you are and reveal
layers of an inner person
and the pain & struggle of that being."

Thank You.

Retired English Teacher
March, 1994

SISTER'S LAMENT

Sometimes I try to step up
To an all-time high
And deliver upon my macho
A spirit –
Me
Then I find myself thinking like you,
For you –
But I am only a man
Attempting to gain sight and security
Through your eyes and heart,
And
This bothers me.
So, with penalty, I release and reveal –
But I can conveniently
Revert back to

me.

L. J. Flood

Blind Acceptance
(In Check)

If only you could
Cry out "foul"
And not be held
Accountable for
Your ignorance.

Like a mile-high
Open charge account,
You let him in
By chance -
> *By chance you did.*

You accepted his pager
And questioned only
His choice of cologne
So now things are moving
Much too fast
Sending all the right
Signals
Sending all the motions
Of hope
Like staring into his face
So convincing
> so bold
While turning
Your frail back

3

L. J. Flood

 To this game of old
He works so much,
Yet you don't see pay,
Can't call him at home
        "He has it that way."

That way - this man
Carrying you like this - like that
Calls upon you
So late
At night
        When he's in the area
And just pops in and
Loves you
Fast.

But still awake,
You dare dream:
"I want this - I want him
To last..."

Then you awaken...
        And see him
                Gone.

No One Knows
(Sister's Lament)

No one knows
Your hurt
Being a man's doormat
So much
Too long
      Seems to be your place.

No one knows

You had a man
With strong arms and big feet
To wipe upon you
While brandishing that love
In his deep
Brown eyes –

Yes, he showed you
Much love,
      Too much love –
A love for you
And any
Weak soul
That fell victim to
His hypnotic spell
Just so he could clean
His dirty soles

L. J. Flood

No one knows

You hurt him in return
But like a man,
He just keeps
Coming back

And like a woman,
          You keep accepting him –
No one knows.

Silence
(When Are You Coming Back?)

Silence
      Is all I hear
Now!
Though the babies cry
And play
And cry
My heart hears
      Silence.

Months gone away
And
Your noise too!

      You sold me on love
Yes!
You bedded me good
Sweated me good
One time, Some time

So now, I sit and bear

      The silence.

The kids
(yours too)

L. J. Flood

All gather about
So young - more innocent
Fearing only the thought
Of not getting ice cream
From the little white truck
Everyday.

Silence

I can still hear
That great rhythmic, melodic squeak
From your big iron bed
That makes me toss
And cry
And wonder why
Now
Silence
     Is all I hear.

Been Bitter At Those Men

Been bitter at those men
that come and go
      so freely
while I am compelled to
stay in my place
so others can say,
"like a lady,"
and yet not say to you,
"like a man."

Been bitter at those men
because many loves long gone
and not one's come through

Been promised a ring so much, and
instead, received those cheap flowers
that you eagerly purchased from that
little *car-chasing* guy at the street light
that same little nothing man
that made you feel
more guilty than I ever could

So you did purchase a bunch of flowers
on the way to my house,
and passed them on to me with
that smooth smile

Been bitter at those same men

L. J. Flood

and you, and
that same
smooth smile
been loved by men
and you
so good
       on schedule
            every Friday
and been abandoned by men

and you
       every Saturday

Been bitter at those same men
that pretend

just like you.

Wanting Him To Leave

Flame's long gone
      Now
Long gone -
Nights come
      Fast
Days too slow
Sleeping with him
Weeping and reaping
What you sow.

No longer in love,
      But loving him -
No longer caring,
      But caring for him.

Seeing this man, day after day -
      Urges on a compelling pain.
Standing out alone cold nights
      Soaking a desperate rain.

Comes home drunk
Raised his hand...
      Once
Cried on your chest...
      Twice.

Too scared to go
Too scared to leave
But just wanting him to
      leave
This *thing* called

Love.

L. J. Flood

Late At Night

That love call comes
so late
when the kids are sound
asleep
      Late at night

You always
mumble something sad
about your troubles

      suppressing me
            depressing me
tilting my guard
yet, undressing me
abruptly,

without finesse

trying, Oh!
trying Oh!
to see you often
seems out of the question
for...
I know what you want
cool, fool man
      late at night
when you get that
urge

For My Woman . . .

I know what you want

    late at night

when a shelf falls
I can't find you –
when the lights blow,
I bump around into
the night
    alone
and the neighbors
threaten
all while
you chase
my big city dreams
    away
and chase any
potential
other love
that I try to build
    away
so that your
interest
can reign
If only
    Late at night.

L. J. Flood

Where Do I Stand?
(She Asked Me)

"Where do I stand?"

She asked me.
In a straightforward way
As I wiped the sweat from my forehead
And rolled *(in my own juices)* away.

"Where do I stand?"

She asked me
      At this time and not before.

*"Now that you have rocked me
As if I were your whore?"*

"Where do I stand?'

She asked me.
      Repeatedly, with a resounding plea.

*"What happens to my life,
Now that you have
Shared your bed with me?"*

I said:

"Nowhere, we're just friends!"

Just Hold Me
(Instead)

Comfort me this early morning.
        Please...
Roll to the left and join me
In a special way.

        Join me...

As I meditate on
An after-night of stress and
Perhaps mess

        Please...

Don't love me by making me love you
        This way
Early on this day
With an ounce of guilt and surrender

        Instead...

Let me unwind myself and
Express
For you and for me
The depth of my desires, and our union
And
Just trust with me and
Realize
A total relief *in this bed*

With far more benefits

        If you'd just hold me
Instead.

L. J. Flood

Two Whole Years
(Three-Hundred, Sixty-Five, Times Two)

Three-hundred, sixty-five, times two
times the wait
times the anticipation
times the sun setting many
times
just to embrace the moon
and the sleepless nights
and the same outcome

a wait -

a type of pain, a mental comfort
a sullen somber sweetness
of patience
down, down, down into the dark passages
of life.

This is a story. Oh yes!

A story about time; a time
sometime
a long time
no hear - no see- no feel - no sweat
no breath stains against your pillow
And.... with only your *own* fragrance to share
and yet
three-hundred, sixty-five, times two

16

you are here, and the days swell
into the nights that carry a symptom
of yesterday's thoughts
and now
you are that road that needs to be
discovered
that path that yearns to be broken

the fork in the divide...
three-hundred, sixty-five, times two
times the wait.

L. J. Flood.

18

BROTHER'S LAMENT

Sometimes I fall so low
And only attract my own image,
But still
I release too few times,
My frailties,
My self-capacity to give,
And then I realize
That I too desire attention.

L. J. Flood

"A man who wanders from the way of understanding will rest in the assembly of the dead."

Proverbs 21:16

L. J. Flood

Maybe It's Me

Maybe it's me
That can't see my own shadow
　　　Though the sun shines bright.

Maybe it's me
That refuses to accept your love
　　　Except at night.

Maybe it's me
That cannot feel the hurt & love
　　　Deep within your soul.

Maybe it's me
Perhaps, and not you,

　　　That's so cold.

L. J. Flood

Take Me

I open myself
and expose my
heart to all that
may harm
and like venom
you burn and
even penetrate
and threaten
my existence

And yet as I
am now
vulnerable
you believe not
in the strength
of your own strength

Let me
enter
but with heed
enjoy
my warmth
my passion
and without
shame or
      sorrow
           or remorse
                  or disrespect
Look at me the
next day
and say

thank you,
    Please come again!

I Need You

I need you

So...

Sing me a song:
            A love anthem
And
Twirl me about
Like the eye
Of a storm...

Embrace me
Ever so
            With my moods,
And calm me
Ever so
for...

I need you.

L. J. Flood

Within Thirty Days

I know that time
When
Your breasts, so tender
And off-limits
Pains from your bra
And your moods swing
Against all
And you put me
Off
No matter how hard I
Try to love you.

And so
Without emotion
You echo your love
For me
While
You turn away
And oftentimes cry
And ache
And pop pain pills
And fake...
While
I wait for you
With you
Within thirty days.

Playing
(With My Heart)

Tempt me in so good
With those big eyes
And that seductive, but phony
Smile -

Sprinkle my clammy flesh
With your quencher
　　　　And then make me suffer
　　　　　　Without you.
Yes! You made me topple my wall
That I prided such in building
Up - way high
Just for people like you.

You tumbled my pride
　　　　You did
Driving me to change my nights
And days,
Making me wait, and want
And pace
With no taste in my mouth
Or in my soul
　　　　Just staring at that phone

You loved me good, but
Just a tad
Selling me your stories of loneliness

L. J. Flood

Of empty moments
And of needing and wanting
     The likes of me.

Then on your answering machine,
You made me leave you message
After message
And probably laughed as you and
Your girlfriends played them all back
While *saying:*

    "Oh! That loved starved fool,
    Listen to his voice. Big man!
    Needs mama. Big man! Now run
    Back, big man
    To another plan "B," no! "C" - but not me.
    Just another face, a voice to play back -
    For I am obviously **not**
    A mere **"man,"** *like you, but rather,*
    In a skirt, and playing, and winning
    And playing
    Like you, and men
    Too often do."

Playing?

Bearing My Child
(There Are No Winners)

Stretching your youthful belly
          beyond
not certain of the future yet to come,
you bore me a child.
though it took acts of love
to start this miracle,
and despite this God-blessing
          I despised you
for making me a father
uninvited.

I cursed you in my heart
for making me
suffer
at night, though
I know very well that you
suffered more
waking at night, singing a lullaby
rocking to sleep
this helpless being
          that *WE* created.

Then waking so early
before the sun
bathing, feeding, mumbling
in your mind
how bad a man, how unfair a man

L. J. Flood

I must be
to not show a care, or bother
to participate
in this whole episode
of parenting

And though I pay and pay
and curse a system
that sees one way
I care so deeply
and wonder where is my child
and pray that blessings are
regarded, and in order for
you, if only for
Bearing my child.

When Dawn Broke
(Without You)

When dawn broke
I was there to greet it.
I had fumbled around much earlier
In the dark
Batting away that pesky fly
From my ear
   Instead of you.

When dawn broke

I saluted the first bird-songs
That preempted the silence
And the veil of the previous
Night's abandon.

When dawn broke

I had experienced several
Nature calls
That compelled me to lie
On my side, and not
On my stomach.
And with this, I did smile
   Without you
Realizing how much still
I was a man
   Without you
When dawn broke.

L. J. Flood

Loved And Lost
(It Is Better To Have...)

I have had
And do regret that
Love passed me
On and on
And left me with
A want, a craving for
A meal
That which is needed
Three times per ⸚

It is such now
That I realize that
Had I not tasted
And nurtured
Perhaps then
I might have
Plunged naively deeper
Into an abyss
      Of denial
Only to later die
An ill-fated, starving
Sort of death
For lack of proper
Sustenance for my
Growth.
So now I want and long
And search
More
Over and under
And over
For yet another
To love and lose
Or keep.

Watercolor Moon

Driving along
Sunday night
following a road so blinding
with city smog
choking my vision
though subdued colors
I do see, there is
no one to understand
the moods that come
like grays on a healthy canvas
none but that moon
that pastel soft
that watercolor moon
shining so dull and
illuminating
this chill of an eve.

This moon, that very moon
that monitors
my every move
my conscience, my night.

so tired of fussing with
her
trying to see it her way
but believing in
mine
so tired of rushing off

L. J. Flood

so fast with
her
on my mind.

speed, speed - rush a corner,
pierce a light -
off so fast, fast
into the night.

driving, driving along
just relying on that
watercolor moon
to remind me
that even in the thick of tension
at dark
I am never too
alone
to cheat, to fool
to fall - to hurt - to heal - to hurt
thanks
   to
     that
       watercolor moon.

I Met A Sister

I met a sister

She knew not of my person
But Instead classified me

She spoke of relations gone, and
Shunned me for
Not being what she had experienced
In a man

I met a sister

Brown, firm
Hued with skin
That foretold
The riches of
The earth

A history
Of mystery
In her eyes
She trusted not herself
And loved me even less
For what she had been told

I met a sister

Who compared me to many

L. J. Flood

And looked beyond me
For a television character
To respect

As I spoke to her
About my dreams
My life
She rebuked me, reduced me
And subsequently
Released me
I met a sister
      But my skin preceded me.

I Tried To Love Her
(In the City Air)

I tried to love her.
With time and thoughts invested

I tried to love her.

With patience and passion
stored in waiting for
her to love me

I tried to love her.

With no loving for yet a year to come

I tried to love her.

Through her temper and tantrums
and many ways
I turned my head
and wept too many times late at night
when she made those delicate decisions
without me, to jump and move away.

I tried to love her.

She just turned me
           on
and

L. J. Flood

      off
like a radio
from weather to talk,
playing slow music then fast.

I tried to convince her that
hope was in my heart
that peace and love
was just around the corner
of a long city block
with lights and sirens
and horns, and short traffic lights
and ambulance trucks racing
and drive-by shootings
and homeless people
at intersections
with elongated faces
with neatly drafted signs around their necks
soliciting spare change -

I tried to love her.

I tried to love her
In pain
       and
In vain.

.

She Wishes Me Tame

She wishes me
tame
With no show of
    Emotion.
Be a man,
And,
Move, not sway.

Speak in a deep
    Resonance
And smile less

Be a man,
and
Challenge a ball game
    Not me... (said she)
But,
Be all you can be.

L. J. Flood

Sometimes
(Make Me See You)

Sometimes I feel
About
For the unknown
Then,
I feel you.

So...
Glance at me
More
And dangle before me
Your bait
And when I bite
Hug me
Then let me go
Then reel me in
No!
Play with me more
Watch me as
I flip and toss
And struggle to
Understand
This hook in my jaw
In my heart
And...
Make me see you
Sometimes.

Brass Man
(Fragile Ego)

Take his already badly
tarnished name
polish it with
fine spun cheese cloth
emotions
like you would
an obscure piece
of dirty brass.
Yes! Buff well
all corners of his fragile
ego
his mind
and watch him begin
to gain sight

and see you

and realize
his true glow
through you.

Polish it - this man
this burned metal of a being
daily
and don't leave him
for one day
unattended
unless you wish him
to tarnish again, again
and again.

L. J. Flood

Dark Sheen

Your dark sheen
Is my weakness

Forever glowing

Haunting me

Your eyes, so piercing
So calm...
      Stripping me
            Rendering me
A frigid bare –

And yet
I enjoy
My nakedness

For you are
Also
My warmth

Your dark sheen.

Care
(That I'm Alone)

You don't care
that I see you
　　　everyday
in my thoughts
on my time
and not yours

you don't feel, or care
that I have
unselfishly surrendered
to this battle
to this fight.

You don't care
that my father's
　　　dead,
my mother's
　　　sick,
my cousin
　　　died,
my uncle is
dying,
my sister's
not talking to me
and that my brother
is having a hard life
　　　every day,

L. J. Flood

and that I chase
away all others
and yet
still support
      your dream *in living color*
while
suspending *in black & white*
my own.
You don't care
      that I am alone.

You Don't Know Me

You don't know me

so don't try
and tell me
your mind
so narrow
with experiences
well hidden.

You don't know me

'cause I like that Jazz
and I nod
and don't blink
on that
beat.

You don't know me

so petty your walk
your talk
no timing
trade a tit
for a tat
and now
it's a spat

You really don't know me.

L. J. Flood

I Know Now

I know now
How it feels
To miss a day...

To not see that
Sun
Rise early
Assuring me
That there is life

I know now
That my heart is
Greater
Than my desire
To see
That new day
And all that
It may bring

I know now that
Neither
The wind
Nor the rumble
Of the quake
Can rival
My confusion

I know now
That
That sun
And that day
Is
You.

Tender
(Falling for a New Love)

I am trying so hard
Not to fall so quickly as she
Trying so hard to shake
The shackles of a previous
Pain
But not wanting to be captured
By this new
Hard-to-believe
Warmth.

Every day that turns,
Finds me more and more
        Vulnerable
And my bare feet and soul,
And tarnished heart
Are sinking in a sea
Of the most potent,
Deepest, love-like challenge
Ever.
All this yet, at a time
When my wounds
Are so very
Open...

Leaving my heart
        Susceptible...

TENDER.

L. J. Flood

My Body, Not My Mind

It's my fault that I chose
to share
        my body
and not
        my mind.

I was not wise; I was not kind.

I led her on by night
and led her astray by day

my way:
        loving life, but not loving life's consequences.

And now, we share
        nothing
but night-life memories
and a precious child
        that has no clue
that I,
a timed-out thoughtless being
        was very much there too.

And now I must continue on
and breathe
stale air and know
in kind

It was indeed my fault
that I chose
to share
        my body
and not
        my mind.

FOR MY WOMAN

Oh! Such silent beings we are–
Such pride on strength –
Never wrong in public
Just depending on you, a woman
But
What a burden lifted, and yet a sweet surrender
To drop all feelings
At your feet
So that you might walk upon them
Like I have enjoyed
For too long in
This man's club of luxury – understand?

L. J. Flood

For My Woman . . .

"The words of a wise man's mouth are gracious, but the lips of a fool shall swallow him up."

Ecclesiastes 10:12

L. J. Flood

Sister's Music
(They Don't Know)

They don't know
My sister's music

They don't know

They don't know
How to soothe
Her ailing spirit,
Her sensitive soul
Her fragile heart
Just soiling her tender
Eardrums
With fake songs
Making her follow
But not leading
Down
      A path of chords

They don't know

The melody, the rhythm
The complex structure
That special harmony
That she needs
And desires
And so they come
Offering

L. J. Flood

Cheap, conniving
Ploys and talk
Just giving her

     A cappella

When she deserves

     A band

They don't know
My sister's music

They don't know.

For My Woman...
And You Thought I Didn't Understand

For my woman...
so dear, so close
with your bed so wet and
soiled;
soiled so deep into the coils
but not with stains
of love -
but rather, with the tears
that you've cried
for all of those cloudy days
that I, a man,
did fail to seek
your touch.

For my woman...
when it was so warm out
I was gone about
abandoning you
for another way -
and I did leave you
on many nights
all alone.
checking on you -
yes! checking
to make sure
you were just that:
alone.

L. J. Flood

For my woman...
I shared those first run
movie scenes with
others,
though I knew
you deserved those moments
more
and I dined in all the right places
with all the wrong faces
all while you
ate carry-out pizza
and sobbed and shared sad songs
with your girlfriends.

For my woman...
I shared my bed with many
and did awaken
most mornings without you
knowing that your fire was
long overdue.
and I called you once,
only after you called me
twice, and some,
and some.

For my woman...
you worked day
and night, and day
sharing your pay
so that I would not fail –

seeing me through thick
times
while yet turning your back
allowing me to cry a lot, not aloud
on my own.

Now, my woman
only that blustery
wind
can carry me
over
and only you
can bring me
back

For my woman...

    I know you thought
        I didn't understand.

L. J. Flood

Caramel

Let me savor your soft touch
As I do admire your entire wrapping
Describing healthy
Ingredients that may
Only urge my desires to want you more -
And it is this urge that causes
Such a confusion to my palate.
Yet, as with all sensual sweet confections,
My tooth calls –

I long to
Suckle this special sweetness through
And through
For, so much more than candy
With a soft creamy center

You are –

Oh now, I must reflect
Not on the times that you
Will consume me more,
But rather on
That smooth skin that meets
Those eyes-
         A wild, magnetic stare:
Brown,
Not almond, but caramel

Staring at me, tempting me,

Assuring me that

Life is

Making me see double – no! Triple.

And now, I pace and stand

Upside -down, over and out

And fear that

As surely as

God's sun sets in the west,

You will, thusly.

Though unlike that sun,

I know you will not rise

To greet me again,

And again,

Or ever,

And I will wilt from

That special craving,

That yearning hunger,

As does

A deserving one

Who has never known

That insatiable

     Taste

    Of

        Caramel.

L. J. Flood

Unfair Love
(Arriving Without You)

Charge me, rev my cold
Male blood
Up   .
Appreciate me
Cause me to be
So proud
That I arrive
Without you
Amidst the passion
Then afterwards
Wipe my brow
And call out loud, then softly
Into the night --

Make sweet chimes as
Only the morning birds dare
Open one eye
And swear,
And pray
That I don't crawl out
Of the warmth, without you --

As with that long
Groan
And tremble
I did arrive same

Without you
Now!
Wait ever so patiently
Yet with concern
For wanting your just
And foster a natural
Anger
And grapple with how terribly
Unfair love is
That you
Did not arrive
Before me.

L. J. Flood

The Woman Star

You are a woman -
No less than the stars
        in the sky.

And I, a man
Moreover
No less than
The moon.

Shifting from full
To crescent
To full again

        I watch you

As you twinkle
With an ethereal brilliance
And form great constellations
        around me.

Yes! You do shoot
Through the heavens
And make people
        wish upon you -
While I exude with luminous pride
And urge
        only the wolves
To sing an eerie howling of a song
        at dark.

You are a woman
        no less than the stars

But far greater than me!

Cinnamon
(A New Spice In My World)

There is a spice
So poignant, so sweet
A place in my imagination
A savory aroma that
Hypnotizes and compels me
Insisting that I break under
And follow you way back to
Tropical Isles by way of Africa
To dwell deep into your
Origins...

Such a brown, brown,
Crying brown
Oh Yes! I saw you first:
Plump, tempting thighs
Conducting the rhythm
Of the hot night's air,
Draped in smooth black
Sheen, clinging like lacquer
Effortlessly
In all the right places.

Now! Disrobe, and expose
Thigh-high, fishnet stockings
Leading way, way up to infinite
Riches -
Natural riches that I long to taste

L. J. Flood

But No!
There you were
Glaring down,
Beaming down on
All of those other
Lost hungry souls
That dwell about
Wanting, but not desiring
Enough to deserve
This queen of all spices

Cinnamon.

One Moment More
(A Rambling Letter)

If for one moment more
I may hold you tight
To my bosom
And show you that which is me:
"That special soul of a man
Who feels a special part of you."

If I could just touch you,
For I know that the charge
Of your lips,
Like that of a nectar,
Is my quench.
And you might see, and feel
That I,
Like your day,
Am real.

I yearn to make you know
That I can feel you, and fill you
With the passion of a small bee
In the midst of
A bounty of honey

I know and hope
To
No longer remain
Hiding in my desires

L. J. Flood

For it is
Your warmth
Your condition
That burns like the
Sun of deepest Africa.
If I could,
I would engulf you
Down, down
Far down
And you will cry out
Into the night
        Into the wind
"It is real,
This tension, this fire -
His fire,
Is hot."

I Have Been There
(Passion)

So tall, so bold
She
      A woman....

And so now
As I am twirled
About
I turn my back
As if to sever
The wind
And its poignant
Sting
From my heart

So strong
Yet fragile
And lost
And foolishly
Helpless

I have been there
Many times
And even as I
Turn away
Like that old moon
On a long
Midnight journey
My feelings
Keep haunting me
Until the next day

I have been there.

L. J. Flood

Leading You On

Never saying

    "Yes!"

Never saying

    "No!"

Just following your lead
Saying
    "Maybe so!"

Empty, open gestures
Like
Returning your calls

    Sometimes -

And disappearing so often
With nothing

(especially not you)
    On my mind.

A Man All Over
(I Yearn To Be Touched)

I yearn
To be touched
To be kissed
To be held
    All over -

My pores are
Open
My knees are
Strong
Make me
A man
    All over -
For...
I yearn
To be touched.

L. J. Flood

Larceny

The moment I begin
to show
      that I care,
that I am for real
you stare at me
      in another light
and make me realize that
familiarity invites
      an ominous contempt.

When you knew me less - so early on
from a distance
so close,
you accepted
      an undiscovered me
and that shadowed your void
and your friends sighed with you
and shared
      your discovery
and urged you on
with your larcenous ways
to ultimately weave
your web
around a man -
that man
      this man
that
certainly deserves
to be kept
      in check...

for your comfort.

Larceny?

Dark Woman
(I Was Lied To)

I, overtaken,
Was lied to
Not knowing that beauty
Was as beautiful
As you...

That sands
Of a cool desert night
Could manifest
Itself in your likeness...

That the calm
Of a retracting tide
Could be
Your entrancing stare...

That polished gold
Was your skin
So rare,
So precious
A gem...

That many
Have fought
Over your
Maternal strength,
Your character,
Your brilliance,
Your resilience to time - your mind...
As pleasant
As the honeysuckle,
Naturally...
I was lied to.

L. J. Flood

You Know
(Discipline)

You know how much
I do like to see you draped
        adorned
        splattered
in those black sheer
soft stockings
with the seam-line
up the middle
and
it does not matter
or distress me
that this dark seam
that so halves
your soft legs, calves
and thighs,
      is off-center
for, your silky sensuousness
      is on

You know
that
my balance - my mind,
my entire purpose
is perplexed - is so distorted-
that my skin boils
with such (sinful) anticipation,
that my eyes water

and itch
with a piercing lust for you -
knowing
that when you lay again
across my lap
and tease,
that I will remain
stable - painfully disciplined
upright
for you
You know, or
Perchance - you don't.

L. J. Flood

Too Often

Too Often
Times
Too often
Moods...

Too often
A mist of
A passion
Unfulfilled...

Day in
Day out
I see through
Closed eyes
And desire deeply
For that
Which is not
Mine
To hold...

Pains that come
Tingling
Even as
I awaken and
Realize that I'm
Lying
Only to
Myself...
Too Often.

Three Roses Came For Me
(How Long Does Love Last?)

Three roses came
for me
on a dismal afternoon.
I saw them there -
so tight, yet so vivid
embellished
with baby-breath
and other greenery
artistically placed in a quaint
cylindrical vase
so tight, with water
and a packet of plant-food
to keep them fresh
to remind me
more
of some new
perhaps near-perfect love
for me.

The deep aqua bow,
cascaded
with a remarkable
semblance
of my own birthstone.

But as in life, with its challenges
I fondled the roses

L. J. Flood

and pricked my finger
on a thorn
and tasted my own
blood
from that wound.

And yet, despite this experience,
for two days
these tokens
stared at me, opening just enough
each day to expose
      a concentrated dose
of the epitome of life -
of nature.

And on day three
I fondled with care
this fragrance
that permeated my senses
that swept me such
as to weep
at the very thought
of those roses
wilting
as all things
in life
      eventually do.

Waiting To Unload
(Like A Time-Bomb)

My love must be
A rare kind
For it remains
Dormant,
Untouched, undiscovered
Like a time bomb
      Ticking
          Waiting
Waiting to explode...

My self expression
My essence
My very touch
      Melts
In a decay...

Waiting to unload.

L. J. Flood

Friend

Long legs
stretching up
and out of
my mind.
with purple hose
        accenting
the silken darkness
prepared by
nature.

Brown skin
like fine milk chocolate
that melts only
        in my dreams.

hurt me good
        but bad
with clothes clad
that cling so well,
but with little effort.

Subtle fragrances
fueling a lust,
encouraging a desire
        to touch
                to share,
to experience the world
of
        My friend.

❈ THANKS ❈

For Inspiration

Nikki Giovanni

Iyanla Vanzant

Audrey Chapman

Oprah Winfrey

Maya Angelou

Zora Neale Hurston

Langston Hughes

L. J. Flood

About the Author

Born and raised in inner-city Washington, DC, Mr. Flood has been writing his form of vivid, metaphor-laced poetry for over twenty-five years. He is a proud member of the Poetry Society of America (PSA), and has authored hundreds of poems, including many theme-related unpublished chapbooks. He currently resides in the suburban Washington, DC metropolitan area with his family, where he enjoys reading, writing and photography.

Thank You For Purchasing My Book!

Need additional copies of
For My Woman...And You Thought I Didn't Understand?

Order your copies exclusively from:

☞ www.1stbooks.com

Do you have comments about the book?
Were you inspired by the writings?
The author would love to hear from you.

Please e-mail all comments to:

☞ ForMyWomanSite@aol.com

Printed in the United States
1220200002B/472-546